LIFE IN A
ROMAN
TOWN

JANE SHUTER

Heinemann
LIBRARY

First published in Great Britain by Heinemann Library, Halley Court, Jordan Hill, Oxford OX2 8EJ, part of Harcourt Education. Heinemann is a registered trademark of Harcourt Education Ltd.

© Harcourt Education Ltd 2005
First published in paperback in 2006
The moral right of the proprietor has been asserted.

Produced for Heinemann Library by Bender Richardson White
Editor: Lionel Bender, Nancy Dickmann, Tanvi Rai
Designer and Media Conversion: Ben White and Ron Kamen
Illustrations: Bill Donohoe, John James and Mark Bergin
Maps: Stefan Chabluk
Picture Researcher: Cathy Stastny and Maria Joannou

British Library Cataloguing in Publication Data
Shuter, Jane
  Life in a Roman town. - (Picture the past)
  937
A full catalogue record for this book is available from the British Library.

Acknowledgements:
The publishers would like to thank the following for permission to reproduce photographs: Ancient Art and Architecture/R. Sheridan pp. **9, 10, 14, 17, 23, 26**; Corbis Images Inc./Araldo de Luca p. **22**; Jane Shuter p. **28**; John Seely pp. **8, 16, 18, 19, 21, 27**; Terry Griffiths/Magnet Harlequin p. **13**; Trevor Clifford p. **12**; Werner Forman Archive pp. **6, 30**; Werner Forman Archive/Museo Nazionale Romano, Rome p. **20**; Werner Forman Archive/Scavi di Ostia p. **25**.

Cover photograph of a Pompeii relief showing coppersmith's workshop reproduced with permission of Ancient Art and Architecture/R. Sheridan.

Every effort has been made to contact copyright holders of any material reproduced in this book. Any omissions will be rectified in subsequent printings if notice is given to the publishers.

Any words appearing in bold, **like this**, are explained in the Glossary.

www.heinemann.co.uk/library
Visit our website to find out more information about **Heinemann Library** books.

To order:
☎ Phone 44 (0) 1865 888066
📄 Send a fax to 44 (0) 1865 314091
💻 Visit the Heinemann Bookshop at www.heinemann.co.uk/library to browse our catalogue and order online.

ABOUT THIS BOOK

This book is about daily life in towns in Roman times. The Romans ruled from about 753 BC to AD 476. At first, they just ruled the city of Rome, in Italy, and the land around it. However, they formed a strong army and a built a huge **empire** by taking over more and more land and ruling it with Roman **laws**. By 265 BC, they controlled most of Italy. Wherever they went, they built towns like those in Italy. The towns were important because the Romans ran the country from them.

We have illustrated this book with photographs of objects and buildings from Roman times. We have also used artists' ideas of town life. These drawings are based on Roman towns that have been found and investigated by **archaeologists**.

The author
Jane Shuter is a professional writer and editor of non-fiction books for children. She graduated from Lancaster University in 1976 with a BA honours degree and then earned a teaching qualification. She taught from 1976 to 1983, changing to editing and writing when her son was born. She lives in Oxford with her husband and son.

Contents

Roman towns

By about AD 100, the Roman **Empire** had spread far and wide. Wherever the Romans went, they took Roman ways with them. New towns were built in the Roman style. The streets were built straight and in a criss-cross pattern. In the town centre, there was an open-air meeting place, the forum. Markets were held here. Usually, there was also a basilica, which was a large building that everyone used. **Officials** ran the area from here. Each town also had **public baths** and toilets and a system of drains and piped water.

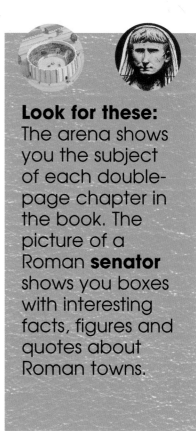

Look for these:
The arena shows you the subject of each double-page chapter in the book. The picture of a Roman **senator** shows you boxes with interesting facts, figures and quotes about Roman towns.

TIMELINE OF EVENTS IN THIS BOOK

753–730 BC The city of Rome is built.

509 BC The Roman army begins to capture lands around Rome.

750 BC	625 BC	500 BC	375 BC	250 BC

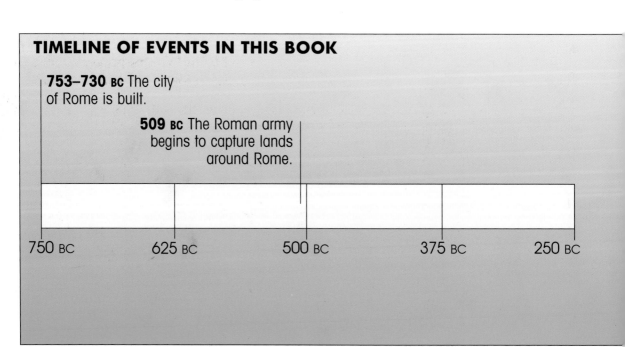

This map shows the Roman Empire at its biggest, in about AD 117. It shows the main towns at that time. Pompeii and Herculaneum, which are the feature of this book, are near Naples, in Italy.

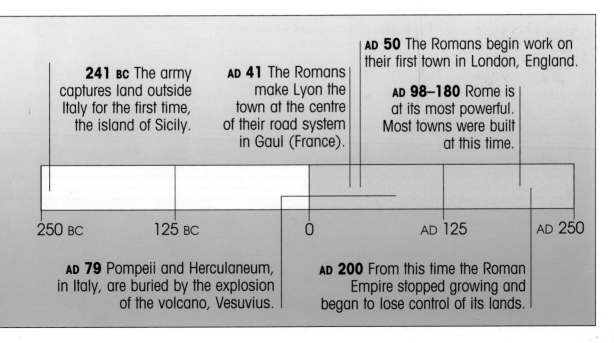

241 BC The army captures land outside Italy for the first time, the island of Sicily.

AD 41 The Romans make Lyon the town at the centre of their road system in Gaul (France).

AD 50 The Romans begin work on their first town in London, England.

AD 98–180 Rome is at its most powerful. Most towns were built at this time.

250 BC   125 BC   0   AD 125   AD 250

AD 79 Pompeii and Herculaneum, in Italy, are buried by the explosion of the volcano, Vesuvius.

AD 200 From this time the Roman Empire stopped growing and began to lose control of its lands.

Who lived where?

A great many people lived and worked in a town. So the town was crowded and noisy, from dawn until late evening. Wealthy people lived in big houses near the edge of town, where it was a little quieter. Craftworkers, such as potters and jewellers, had shops near the forum. They usually lived above their shops. The main roads in and out of towns were lined with tombs of the wealthy.

This is just one end – the eastern end – of the forum in Rome. The building with the little dome, on the left, is a **temple**. The big arches behind it are the remains of a basilica, one of the biggest in the forum.

TOWN BASICS

Every town had at least:

- an open-air meeting place, the forum
- offices for the **officials** who ran the area
- at least one basilica
- a temple
- **public baths**
- shops and inns.

Workers with noisy, smelly jobs – leather makers, butchers and metal workers – lived in the poorer part of town. Here, the streets were narrower and the buildings higher. Many people lived crammed into buildings like blocks of flats. The poorest people of all wandered the streets begging and slept in doorways at night.

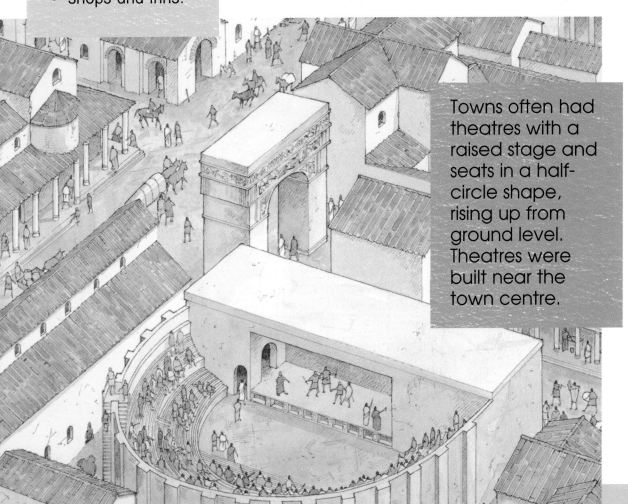

Towns often had theatres with a raised stage and seats in a half-circle shape, rising up from ground level. Theatres were built near the town centre.

The forum

The forum was an open-air space, usually in the middle of a town. It was used for meetings and markets. All around the forum were important buildings. There were **temples** to Roman gods and goddesses. There were the basilicas from where **officials** ran the country and organized what went on in the town. The officials had to make sure drains worked and the markets were run properly.

This is part of the forum of Pompeii, in Italy. The column on the far right is where the temple of Jupiter, god of the sky, stood. The paved area between that and the next set of columns had a roof to make a shady walkway.

The **law** courts were also in the basilica building. When the lawyers and officials were not using the basilica, it was used for markets or public meetings. People, mostly men, also came to the forum to chat, find work or arrange a marriage or a business deal. Women and children, especially from rich families, mainly stayed at home. The roads into the forum were packed with people and slow, heavy carts carrying goods to be sold or **traded**.

Rich **senators** like these, met in the forum to talk business. They also ruled the **empire**, until emperors took over, from 27 BC. When they ran the empire they did all their decision making in a building at the forum.

The baths

All towns had **public baths**. Here people could wash, bathe, swim and exercise. Some towns had several public baths, each with different entry charges depending on what they provided. The cheapest public baths just had a changing room and three connecting rooms, kept at different temperatures. There was a cold room with a cold pool; a warm room where bathers oiled and scraped themselves clean; and a hot room with a hot pool.

The entrance halls to baths, like this one, had rooms running off right and left. They were often important meeting places for bathers, with a fountain and seating areas.

Romans bathed naked, and oiled and scraped themselves clean – there was no soap. More expensive public baths had **saunas**, open-air pools and **slaves** to clean and massage the bathers. Some towns had public baths just for women and girls, or just for men and boys. Other baths were open to men, women or families at different times of the day.

NOISY NEIGHBOURS

The Roman writer Seneca lived opposite a public bath: 'I hear all the groans and grunts of people exercising, or pretending to. I hear the slapping sounds of people being massaged. Then there are those who like to sing, or dive in loudly. The noise of people having their armpits plucked is awful.'

Some public baths provided food and drink, such as bread, cheese, fruit, water and wine. Walls, floors and ceilings were decorated with mosaics and paintings.

11

The games

Most towns had a circus (an oval trackway for **chariot** racing) and an arena for games. Towns with a circus had several chariot racing teams that people supported just as people support football teams now. Each team had a different colour that their drivers, horses and supporters wore. Men, women and children, rich and poor, all went to the circus to cheer their teams.

The Colosseum in Rome was the biggest arena in the Roman world. It could hold 45,000 people sitting, with another 5000 standing. On hot, sunny days there was a system of awnings to shade most of the seats.

Most shows in the arena were fights between gladiators and animals or each other. There were different teams of gladiators, each part of a different gladiator 'school' that trained them in different ways of fighting. Sometimes, pairs of gladiators fought until one of them was killed. Many gladiators were prisoners who were due to die anyway and could live longer – or gain their freedom – if they fought and won.

GLADIATORS

There were different kinds of gladiators:

- a *retiarius* fought with a net, to trap his opponent, and a three-pointed spear called a trident
- a *Samnite* fought with a sword and wore armour, including a helmet and a big shield
- a *Thracian* fought with a dagger, wore some body armour and carried a small, round shield.

This expensive drinking cup was decorated with a painting of gladiators. It was sent to England from Germany.

Temples

The Romans worshipped many gods and goddesses, and towns had **temples** to the most important ones. Temples were houses for statues of the gods. Valuable presents given to the gods were stored there. Only the **priests** and **priestesses** who served the gods went into temples. Ordinary people waited just outside temples on special days, where **religious ceremonies** were held.

WHO PAID?

Temples were expensive to build. Wealthy people often had them built as a thank you to the gods for a favour. Sometimes the people who ran each town decided to build a temple. The money came from the **taxes** that everyone had to pay.

These priests are holding an open-air ceremony for the goddess Isis. She was an Egyptian goddess, but the Romans added her to their gods and goddesses when they took over Egypt.

Ordinary people worshipped at **shrines** set up in towns and in the countryside. Every home also had a small shrine, where the family worshipped the gods and goddesses who looked after the house. Roman prayers were usually a bargain with a particular god or goddess. They offered them a gift and expected the gods to do something in return.

Most temples had:
- a grand entrance, with steps up and columns that held up carved stonework and an inverted V-shaped roof
- no windows and just one door
- an altar used by the priests at festival times
- statues to the gods and goddesses.

The theatre

Townspeople went to the theatre often. The theatre was open-air, with a stage and a semi-circular seating area. The audience sat on stone benches that went up in steps. Women and young children had to sit separately from the men. Plays were either funny comedies or tragedies, where things turned out badly. Many plays were put on as part of **religious festivals** and **ceremonies,** and were performed to please the gods.

This theatre in Pompeii, Italy, held about 5000 people. The biggest theatre of all, in Rome, held 27,000. The prices of seats varied – the cheapest were at the top.

All the actors in the theatre were men. They wore different masks to show what kind of person they were playing. Brown masks were for men, white for women. The masks had different expressions, too. Musicians played pipes, banged drums and shook tambourines during the play, making the music sad or happy to fit what was happening on stage.

The actors in this mosaic are shown in their dressing room – a big space behind the stage. The actors have **slaves** to help them change, something only large theatres could afford.

Homes

In towns, ordinary family homes were built two storeys high, with rooms facing inwards to an **atrium** or courtyard. The atrium was open to the sky, often with a pool in the middle to catch rainwater and a covered walkway all around at ground level. The rooms on the ground floor opened on to the atrium. Craftworkers' homes had a shop open to the street, so passers-by could buy the things they made.

Wealthy people often had a garden at the back of their town house, like this one. The garden had a **porch** running all around it to give shade in summer and shelter from the rain in winter.

Poorer townspeople lived in two- or three-storey buildings like blocks of flats, called *insulae*. A whole family might share one room. They lived, ate, cooked on a fire and slept in the room. Most *insulae* did not have toilets or piped water. Also, they were badly built and, because they were crammed together and had wooden beams and floors, they were a big fire risk. The poorer areas of towns burned down regularly.

ALL FALL DOWN?

The Roman writer Juvenal was talking about the *insulae* of Rome when he said: 'Most of the city is propped up with planks of wood to stop it falling down. The landlord says "sleep well" when he knows you will be lucky if the building stays up through the night.'

Homes like this one, that had walls on the street, often had only small windows with metal bars set in them on the street side. This was to keep the houses safe from burglars.

Work

In Roman times, women married and ran the home. They shopped, cooked and raised their children, or had **slaves** to do this for them. Men went out to work. Wealthy men did not work, but left the house to do various kinds of business, such as buying and selling slaves. Craftworkers had workshops, and sold **goods** from there or at markets in the forum. **Traders** had offices near the docks, where there were also warehouses to store the goods they bought and sold.

This carving shows a shoemaker and his assistant in their workshop. The shoemaker kept a few sizes of the types of shoe he made in a cupboard. People chose a style from his stock, then he measured their feet and made the shoes to fit exactly.

WOMEN AT WORK

Married women from wealthy families spent their time entertaining or making sure slaves ran the home properly. Those from poor families had to work, helping their husbands. If their husbands died, women sometimes took over and ran their businesses.

Towns were so full of shoppers that poorer people could sell things without owning a shop. They sold fruit, vegetables and cooked food – including cakes and sausages – from stalls on the streets, or even from baskets on their heads! Other poor people worked for builders or traders, carrying heavy loads, storing goods or mixing cement. They also worked in the inns and eating places, as cooks, cleaners or waiters.

Some people, like the musicians and actors in this mosaic, made a living performing in the street. After a performance, they collected money from people who had stopped to watch their show.

Schools

Children did not have to go to school in Roman times, but some did. There was no free education and no special school buildings. Good teachers charged high fees and hired a room to teach in, often in the basilica. Other teachers charged less, but could not afford to hire a room. They taught in courtyards or shop doorways. Their classrooms were open to the street and all its distractions. Some were even on the pavement.

SCHOOL TIME

Every day was a school day, except for a break of eight days in the summer. Lessons started at dawn and went on until midday. There was a lunch break, then school began again until about 3 p.m.

Children at an expensive *ludus* wrote with pens and ink, and with a sharp-pointed stick and slabs of wax melted into a wooden case. Poorer children used reed pens and scraps of paper. This carving shows a tutor writing on a slab of wax.

There were two kinds of school: the *ludus* – for girls and boys aged 7 to 10 – and the *grammaticus* – for boys from 11 to 15. Only boys from well off families went to a *grammaticus*. The work was very dull. They learned long sections of Roman and Greek writings off by heart. Some wealthy parents hired a tutor to teach their children at home. These children might also learn music and art.

The sons of craftworkers sometimes went to a *ludus*, but then they left school and learned a **trade**, like the metalworkers' sons seen here. When girls left school, they helped their mothers at home.

Clothes

Poor townspeople made their own clothes, spinning wool and weaving it into cloth. People with money to spare could buy cloth ready made from weaving shops. For coloured cloth, they went to dyeshops. Cloth was dyed (coloured) with plant material, or even crushed insects!

Roman men and women all wore a **tunic** and a strip of cloth that was wrapped around their waist and tucked between their legs. They wore layers of tunics and lengths of cloth over these, depending on how hot it was.

Slaves or the women of the house sometimes washed underwear and things that needed special care in rainwater from the **atrium**. But most things, especially sheets, were sent to a laundry. Here, washing was done in big stone baths. Some laundries had heated rooms for drying when the weather was bad.

Children wore a *bulla*, a good-luck charm, around their necks, as in this carving. They were given it when they were born and it was one of the things they gave to the gods in the **ceremony** where they became adults.

Wealthy people had the biggest choice of cloth and clothing. They could buy wool or linen, usually dyed in the most expensive colours. They were the only people who could afford silk brought from the East. Wealthy men often wore a toga – a half-circle of cloth draped round the body. Wealthy women had their clothes made for them by dressmakers.

Shopping

In Roman towns you could buy almost anything, from cooking pots to sandals. Shops had a room opening on to the street, with a workspace behind where the **goods** were made. If the shopkeeper did not have what the customer wanted, he made it specially. Not all shopkeepers made the things they sold. Some shops sold beautiful, expensive jewellery, painted glass and decorated pottery brought from other countries.

Roman butchers cut their meat into joints, then sold it by weight, just like a modern butcher. You can see the weighing scale to the right of the butcher in the picture.

MARKET DAY

Markets were usually held in the forum several times a week, sometimes daily. Shopkeepers sometimes had a market stall. But the market was mainly for fresh foods such as fruit, vegetables, milk and cheese. These had to be bought daily as there were no refrigerators to keep things cold.

Townsfolk were not the only people to shop in towns. People came shopping from villages and **villas** all around. They came to buy things that they could not get locally. They sometimes also came to sell things at the town markets. Towns were especially noisy and busy on market days. The streets, crowded even on normal days, had to cope with carts and animals being driven to and from market.

Shops had a wide opening, which could be shut off with a wooden shutter, and a door. Goods were usually displayed on a table and hanging from hooks above it. The **porch** sheltered the customers and the goods.

Eating out

Most wealthy Romans ate at home, or at the homes of their friends. They ate mostly meat and fish stews, cooked over an open fire. They dined out when they were travelling, in inns or taverns where they hired a room to themselves. The men snacked or drank in town bars. Most eating places sold cheap food to travellers or people who had no kitchens to cook in. The food included olives, sausages, chicken wings, bread and cheese.

Food shops were often on street corners, like this one. This gave them two counters on to the street. Food and drink was kept warm or cool in pottery containers (bottom left), set into the counter, and sold by the bowl or glass. Customers stood at the counter.

A Roman recipe – fish sauce

The Romans used this fish sauce in the way many people use tomato paste now. They put a spoonful of it in almost anything they were cooking. They also spread it on warm toast as a snack or a starter before a meal.

WARNING: Do not cook anything unless there is an adult to help you. Always ask an adult to open cans.

You will need:
85 g of unsalted anchovies or sardines, tinned in olive oil
1 tablespoon vinegar
1 teapoon olive oil
1 clove of garlic, crushed
1/2 teaspoon pepper
1 teaspoon dried mixed herbs
a clean, dry glass jar with a lid.

1 Open the can of fish and put it, with the oil, into a mixing bowl.

2 Mash up the fish with a fork until it is mushy.

3 Add the garlic and mash up again until you cannot tell what is fish and what is garlic.

4 Add the vinegar, pepper and herbs and stir gently until it is all mixed in.

5 Spoon the mixture into the jar and leave in the fridge for two days.

Some modern towns, such as London (in England), Rome (in Italy) and Lyons (in France) have been lived in ever since Roman times. Some still have buildings from Roman times, such as the Colosseum in Rome. Some Roman towns are not used now, but have survived for us to visit. Of these, the most famous and best preserved are Pompeii and Herculaneum in southern Italy, buried by the eruption of a volcano in AD 79.

Pompeii – shown here – and Herculaneum were kept safe under the ash from the volcano. From the 1750s, people have **excavated** the towns. Ever since they have been open to the weather and weeds, preserving them has been a problem.

Glossary

archaeologist person who uncovers old buildings and burial sites to find out about the past

atrium courtyard, open space within a house

chariot platform on wheels, pulled by horses

empire a country and all the other lands it controls

excavate dig out and remove items from the ground

goods things that are made, bought and sold

laws rules made by the people who are running the country. People who break these rules are punished.

official person who helps run an empire or part of it

porch roofed area to give shelter on the outside wall of a house

priest/priestess man/woman who works in a temple, serving a god or goddess

public baths town baths that everyone can use

religious ceremony/festival special time or event when people go to one place to pray to a god or goddess

sauna rest room in which water is poured on hot stones to make steam

senator important and wealthy man in the Roman Empire

shrine place where people go to pray to gods and goddesses and leave them gifts

slaves people who are bought and sold like property. They cannot leave their owners, but may be given or allowed to buy their freedom

tax money that people living in a country have to pay to help run the country

temple place where people pray to gods and goddesses

trade this can mean: **1** a job, for example making shoes or clothes **2** selling or swapping goods, for instance the Romans traded oil for wheat

tunic item of clothing similar to a long T-shirt

villa large house in the country or by the sea. Villas often had farms too, where crops and animals were raised.

More books to read

History of Britain: Roman Britain, Brenda Williams (Heinemann Library, 1997)

See Through History: Ancient Rome, Simon James (Heinemann Library, 1996)

The Life and World of Julius Caesar, Struan Reid, (Heinemann Library, 2002)

Visiting the Past: Pompeii and Herculaneum, John and Elizabeth Seely (Heinemann Library, 1999)

Index